This journal belongs to:

MW00949171